READING

Teacher's Book

**Don McGovern, Margaret Matthews
and S. E. Mackay**

New York London Toronto Sydney Tokyo Singapore

PRENTICE HALL INTERNATIONAL ENGLISH LANGUAGE TEACHING

First published 1994 by
Prentice Hall International (UK) Ltd
Campus 400, Maylands Avenue
Hemel Hempstead
Hertfordshire, HP2 7EZ
A division of
Simon & Schuster International Group

Typeset in 11/12 Garamond
by Fakenham Photosetting Limited

Printed and bound in Great Britain by
Redwood Books, Trowbridge, Wiltshire

British Library Cataloguing in Publication Data

A catalogue record for this book is available from the British Library

ISBN 0–13–303710–X ✓

1   2   3   4   5   98   97   96   95   94

CONTENTS

INTRODUCTION

The Reading component of the series English for Academic Study represents a task-based approach to reading which includes a considerable degree of focus on language form. The course contains seven units. The estimated teaching time for the entire book is roughly between 40 and 60 hours, depending on the needs and language proficiency of the group and the selectiveness teachers wish to exercise in going through the units.

These materials have benefited from extensive trials and evaluation on pre-sessional courses at the Centre for Applied Language Studies, University of Reading. Both tutors and students have contributed significantly to the improvement of the course during its four years of development.

The Reading course can be used either on its own or in conjunction with the Writing course in this series. If you decide to use the Reading book on its own, there is a gradual progression from reading to writing so that students can make use of some of the content of the reading texts and produce the features of language use seen in the tasks. If the Writing course is being used in conjunction with the Reading course, there are suggestions to the teacher on how to approach the Reading essay so that it will not seem to repeat the work done in the Writing course.

Integration of Reading and Writing courses

A unique feature of the series is the integration of corresponding units in the Reading and Writing courses in two aspects:

1. subject content
2. rhetorical functions and features of language use.

The following outline will make this clear:

Reading topic	Common functions/features	Writing topic
1. Academic success	Readership Text organisation	1. Writing about writing
2. Counselling overseas students	Argument Degree of certainty	2. Studying abroad
3. Urban development	Comparison/contrast	3. Comparing and contrasting cities
4. Global warming	Situation/problem/solution Definition	4. Global warming
5. Education in Asia	Extended definition	5. Your academic subject
6. International diplomacy	Situation/problem/solution	6. International tourism
7. Development and cultural values in Africa	Argument Degree of certainty	7. International students

INTRODUCING THIS BOOK

How to use this reading course

To provide a sound basis for the development of reading strategies and skills, it is suggested that you go through the chapter 'Introducing this book' in the Student's Book thoroughly with students. They will need to understand the aims and approach of the course, which may be new to them, and to have a coherent grasp of the nature and purpose of the different strategies and skills. It would be useful to remind them at frequent intervals of the practical application of these during their academic courses, so that they see the immediate purpose of what they are learning.

They will also need to become fluent in the use of the metalanguage outlined in this chapter of the Student's Book. This fluency is intended to aid their awareness of their own development in reading. To further this development, in certain places they are asked to identify which reading skill(s) they have practised in particular exercises. It is suggested that you do this at more frequent intervals than is indicated in the Student's Book.

It is important to emphasise that the reading materials:

(a) cover a variety of topics
(b) are of general interest
(c) contain sub-technical vocabulary common to many fields.

Some students may feel that the topics do not relate directly enough to their particular subject areas. Others may feel initially that some of the topics are too 'technical'. You can point out that this book is designed for students in a wide range of academic subjects – arts, social sciences and sciences. For that reason, the effort has been made to choose 'common denominator' subjects which would be of general interest to an educated readership.

An effort has also been made to avoid subjects which may be perceived as too culturally specific – i.e. too specific to Western cultural and educational conditions. Inevitably, however, the approaches taken by particular writers to particular subjects are in varying degrees culturally bound. In cases in which this is very apparent, however, an effort has been made to focus the attention of students on this factor as a possible limitation. In Unit 1, for example, the discussion questions ask whether the concepts of learner independence outlined in the text are too culturally bound and whether they would be acceptable in the students' own countries. Cultural factors may also lead some students to question the relevance, for example, of global warming, but this has become a widely discussed international issue, especially since the Rio Conference in June 1992.

It would be a good idea to ask students to read the chapter 'Introducing this book' as homework before you take it up in class, or as consolidation.

THE ESSAY

The writing tasks at the end of each Reading unit are designed to enable students to put into practice some of the features of organisation, language use and rhetorical function which have been highlighted in the exercises. They are also intended to consolidate and extend the students' knowledge of the subject content in the texts.

It is recommended that you assign these essays to be done under timed conditions. The experience of writing under time constraints will prepare students for the 'real' conditions of tests and examinations which many will face on an academic course. This approach will complement the methodology of the Writing book, which has a strong emphasis on writing as process and no emphasis on timed conditions.

Decisions will then need to be made about whether you want students to write one, two or more drafts of the essay, and how you want them to plan the work before writing.

If you decide to assign the essay under timed conditions, the maximum recommended time is 60 minutes. More proficient groups can be given 45–50 minutes. In any event, it would help to give the students a guideline of at least 10 minutes for planning before they start writing. In this case they should write *one* draft only. Emphasise that they should be strict with themselves about the time limit if the essay is written as homework. In the early stages of the course you may want to do one or more of these essays on a timed basis in class, so that students become accustomed to the time limit. Some will probably request this.

Reading strategies and skills

You may want to present students with a useful distinction between strategies and skills. A strategy can be described as the conscious application of a particular reading method, and a skill can be presented as an acquired strategy. In other words, a skill is a strategy which can be practised with ease and fluency, which has become 'second nature'. Look at the list of strategies and skills in the Student's Book.

1. Predicting, skimming and scanning

One approach here would be to ask students how these first three reading strategies relate to each other, or what they have in common. Essentially, they all relate to the first stages of the reading process. They are initial strategies designed to form a preliminary sense of what a text contains. They can be contrasted with detailed reading.

2. Detailed reading

This can be characterised as the second stage of the reading process, in which one reads for secondary ideas and details as well as for further clarification of main ideas. It may involve a second or third reading of a text. This stage can be further contrasted with predicting, skimming and scanning above. Reading speed is an important difference between these first and second stages.

3. Understanding main ideas and text organisation

These two strategies can also be linked. Identifying main ideas can be presented as a first step in understanding the way in which a text is organised. Refer students again to Section 2, 'Skimming', in 'Introducing this book', where the most usual locations of main ideas in a text are specified.

4. Understanding text organisation, assessing a writer's purpose and evaluating a writer's attitude

The connection between these three is made clear in the Student's Book. A writer's purpose will be one of the factors determining his or her method of organisation. This in turn will be one of the ways in which a writer reveals a particular attitude or bias.

You may want to outline the relationship between purpose and attitude in this way:

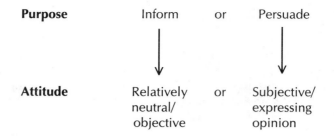

Purpose	Inform	or	Persuade
Attitude	Relatively neutral/ objective	or	Subjective/ expressing opinion

It is important to emphasise the importance of 'relatively' in describing a writer's attitude as neutral. Very few texts can demonstrate entire objectivity in presenting information.

Evaluate is a key word here and in the Writing course in this series. You may want to ascertain and clarify the students' understanding of this word. It can be described as the effort to assess or analyse the value or degree or amount of something; the attempt to exercise critical judgement. In this case, students will assess the degree of bias or opinion presented by a writer.

 # Sample reading text

TASK 1. SKIMMING AND PREDICTING

1.1 It would be a good idea here to go carefully through the labelled parts of the article and explain how each one can provide important information about the usefulness or relevance of the article for a reader's needs.

TASK 2. UNDERSTANDING MAIN IDEAS

2.1 Answers to summary:

    (a) fibre
    (b) white bread and white rice
    (c) resistant starch

At this point you may want to illustrate the differences between technical and sub-technical vocabulary in relation to this text, as follows:

1. Ask students to identify the first instance of *technical vocabulary* used in the text. This is **resistant starch** (line 27). Emphasise that this term is explained in its initial context because of its technical nature.

2. Ask students to identify the first instance of *sub-technical vocabulary* in the text. This is probably **dietary fibre** (line 3). Point out that it is not explained initially

because the writer assumes that educated general readers will be familiar with it.

3. Place headings for two columns on the board:

Technical vocabulary   **Sub-technical vocabulary**
resistant starch (lines 19, 27, etc)   dietary fibre (line 3)

Ask students to find *at least three* more examples of each form of vocabulary. They can work in groups of two or three. The completed list would look something like this:

Technical vocabulary	Sub-technical vocabulary
resistant starch (lines 19, 27, etc.)	dietary fibre (line 3)
amylose starch/polymers (lines 101, 104–5)	carbohydrate (line 12)
	cellulose (line 21)
crystallites (line 106)	diverticulosis (line 38)
butyric acid (line 145)	digestive enzymes (line 83)
amylopectin (line 150)	molecular structures (lines 107–8)
	hydrogen bonds (lines 108–9)
	genetic engineering (lines 153–4)

After doing this exercise students can begin to realise that the vocabulary in this text is not as difficult as it may seem initially. All of the technical terms on the left are explained in the context, although it could be argued that the explanations of **amylose starch** and **amylose polymers** are insufficient for educated general readers unless they have a specific interest in science or nutrition.

The terms on the right are not explained, however, because the author assumes that his readers will have at least some understanding of them. The only exception to this is **fibre**, which is given a fuller explanation in a later context (lines 45–7). Some readers may feel that **diverticulosis** is more technical than sub-technical, but the term is now used in texts relating to nutrition and health and is not explained in detail here. You may want to omit this word from the list.

TASK 3. EVALUATING A WRITER'S PURPOSE AND ATTITUDE

3.1 (a) Most of the text is devoted to presenting information on this subject. However, you may want to ask students to search the text for specific attempts to persuade readers to accept a point of view. In lines 158–62 the writer expresses a clear opinion about the issue described in lines 118–23. The writer clearly sides, in other words, with those scientists who regard resistant starch as a form of fibre. He therefore makes some attempt to persuade as well.

You can make the point here that many texts both inform and persuade. It is often a matter of evaluating which of the two purposes is the dominant one.

(b) The author probably has a good knowledge of this subject because of:

- the detailed information contained in the article, presented in a coherent way
- his credentials as a chemist at a reputable academic institution
- his authorship of a book on the subject published by a leading academic press.

(c) This may provoke some interesting discussion. We hope that the author is not motivated by vested interest, but we do not know. Given the fact that scientific funding in university departments sometimes comes from commercial sources, however, this is not impossible.

TASK 4. A READER'S PURPOSE

You may want to point out that another way of thinking about a reader's purpose is to ask about his or her motivation for reading.

4.1 Readers (b) and (c) would probably have the most practical interest in reading the article. Reader (d) would be most likely to have an intellectual interest.

4.2 Answers can vary here. It can be argued that readers (a) and (b) would be more likely to skim. Reader (b) may also want to scan for practical advice related to shopping.

Readers (c) and (d) may be more likely to read the article thoroughly because of their greater knowledge of and interest in the subject.

UNIT

ACADEMIC SUCCESS

The topic and text in this unit are designed to prepare students for some of the assumptions and ideas involved in the concept of *learner independence*. In most English-medium universities this will be expected of students undertaking degree courses. Students from non-Western educational backgrounds may need some preparatory work for this unit, perhaps in the form of a discussion of how cultural differences are reflected in approaches to education.

If you are using the Writing book in this series, these texts will also help to prepare students for some of the ideas behind the 'writing as process' approach.

 Text 1.1

TASK 1

1.1 Intelligence

TASK 2

2.2 Two

2.3 **Twenty years ago** (line 1), **Today** (lines 10, 21)

They are emphasised in the first and second paragraphs by being placed in the opening position. It could be pointed out that adverbial words and phrases can be emphasised by being placed:

(a) at the opening of a paragraph
(b) at the beginning of a sentence.

2.4 Try to elicit examples and ask whether they work in the text as it stands; for example:

At that time	in those days	in the past	before	previously, etc.
now	nowadays	at present	at the present time, etc.	

Not all of these could replace the time indicators in the text, however. 'In the past' could replace **Twenty years ago**, and 'before' and 'previously' would work to some extent. However, the other synonyms for **Twenty years ago** would not work because of the reference items 'that' and 'those'.

2.5 They serve as the basis of the text organisation and create a 'vertical' pattern of contrast (see Unit 3). Paragraph 1 = **Twenty years ago** and paragraphs 2 and 3 = **Today**. The effect is to highlight the contrast between accepted views then and now.

It may also be helpful to focus on the different use of tenses for each time period, if the proficiency level of the group seems to warrant it.

TASK 3

You may want to remind students of the terms *immediate context* and *wider context* from the chapter 'Introducing this book' in the Student's Book, to bring out concrete strategies for guessing these words. In each case students can be asked whether they used:

(a) the immediate context
(b) the wider context
(c) their own knowledge of the subject

to help them guess the meaning.

3.1   1. (b)   2. (a)   3. (b)   4. (c)   5. (a)   6. (b)   7. (c)

The contexts of 1, 2, 5 and 6 give relatively little help in guessing the meanings of these words. It could be pointed out that *in other contexts* the words in Task 3 could have other definitions than those given above; for example:

1. **orientations** (a)
2. **motivations** (in the form 'motive', adj) (b)
4. **speculate** (a)
6. **arousal** (usually in the form 'arouse', vb) (a)
7. **application** (a) and (b)

TASK 4

Some introduction to the functions of *generalisation* and *qualification* will probably be necessary here, depending on the needs and level of your group.

You may want to elicit examples of generalisation and list them on the board/OHP. Students, working either in pairs or in plenary, can then be asked to qualify these so that they become both more specific and more tentative in their assertions. One example of a generalisation would be:

Physical fitness is the most important factor in athletic performance.

Students can then be asked to qualify this statement. One result would be:

There is evidence to suggest that physical fitness **can be considered one of the most** important factors in athletic performance.

The generalisation has been qualified in four ways:

1. Reference is made to evidence (although it is not specific – ask students to improve on this).
2. **to suggest** is more tentative.
3. **can be considered** is more tentative than **is**.
4. **one of** further qualifies or limits the statement in terms of number.

4.1 1. [**Teachers … would have mentioned**] **the effects of interests other than academic ones** (lines 4–5)
2. **they would have mentioned study methods** (line 7)
3. **their answers would have depended on observation and personal belief** (line 8)

If students seem to have trouble identifying generalisations, you may want to continue this exercise by asking them to identify others in the second paragraph.

4.2 **very probably** (line 4)   **Possibly** (line 7)   **In any case** (line 7)
more likely (line 11)   **possible** (line 18)   **less likely** (line 21)

Compare also **might speculate** (lines 17–18) and other conditional verb uses to qualify generalisations in this text.

You may also want to focus on **usually** (line 25) and to highlight other forms of expression commonly used to qualify generalisations; for example:

Quantity	**Frequency**	**Probability (adverbs/adjectives and verbs)**	
all	always	certain/ly	will
many	often	probable/ly	would
few	sometimes	perhaps	might etc.

Students can be asked to contribute other items to this list, in a position corresponding to their relative degree of quantity/frequency/probability.

Task 5

5.1 No. The conclusion is too unqualified.

5.2 Possible answer is:

> *Research involving students in British sixth forms and colleges suggests that intelligence bears/may bear little or no relation to academic performance.*

Similar versions are acceptable. You may want to place the different versions proposed by two or three students on the board/OHP and discuss in plenary whether or not they are sufficiently qualified. The version above can then be added, if it is significantly different from the students' versions. Students can then be asked how many qualifying features or elements the statement contains (underlined above):

1. The research was carried out only in Britain.
2. It involved only students in sixth forms and colleges.
3. The tentative verb 'suggests' has been used.
4. 'may bear' further qualifies the verb use.
5. 'little or no relation' qualifies the original **no relation**.

It would be helpful at this point to explain the importance of these functions in academic writing generally, especially the *degree* to which statements are qualified and the *degree of certainty* which this implies. Other exercises on degree of certainty in various forms are found in Units 2 and 7.

5.3 It is restricted to sixth forms and colleges in Britain. It may be helpful to focus on and explain the key words **highly selected** (line 23).

 # Text 1.2

Task 6

6.1 **Levels of maturity and students' expectations. Cognitive styles** would be a reasonable second choice. It will help to make the discussion more concrete if students are asked to refer to specific parts of the text to support their views.

> It would be useful to explain in Text 1.2:
>
> (a) The use of inverted commas in lines 5, 24, 25, 42 and 44
> (b) The use of verbs like **realised** in line 50 which presuppose the truth of what follows. You may want to elicit synonyms such as 'recognised', 'understood', 'became aware that', etc.

Task 7

7.1 Stage 1: **In a first stage, he found that students expected to find the 'right answers' which were known to 'Authority' and saw it as Authority's role to teach these answers to students.** (lines 23–6)

Stage 2: **Thus, they either assumed that in the absence of an absolute Authority no meaningful judgements could be made, or sought to maintain dependence on Authority and 'absolute truths', since without them they would feel, as one student put it: 'If everything is relative, nothing is true, nothing matters'.** (lines 44–9)

[Lines 39–44 provide an equally effective summary, but they consist of two sentences.]

Stage 3: **By the third stage, Perry found that students realised that knowing and valuing were relative in time and circumstances and that an individual was faced with responsibility for choice and commitment in life.** (lines 50–3)

Task 8

8.1 Perry (1968) is the main source.
Gibson (1970)
Peters (1958)
Veness (1968)

> It may be useful to clarify here what is usually meant by *sources* or *references* in academic language and what these terms can include:
>
> 1. Academic books and textbooks
> 2. Articles in academic journals
> 3. Some articles in quality newspapers and magazines
> 4. Published/unpublished papers given at academic conferences
> 5. Published/unpublished monographs and dissertations
> 6. Published/unpublished letters
> 7. Recorded interviews.

Task 9

It would be useful to elicit the students' understanding of *synonym* and *antonym* before doing this exercise.

synonym = a word (or phrase) that is similar or closely similar in meaning to another in the same language.

antonym = a word (or phrase) that is opposite in meaning to another in the same language.

9.1　　1. (a)　2. (c)　3. (a)　4. (b)　5. (c)　6. (b)　7. (a)

9.2　　
1. worried	3. finding	5. reverting	7. compared to
2. power	4. preserve	6 supporting	

> In this task and in other vocabulary exercises involving synonyms and antonyms in this book, it is suggested that you take time to explain some of the differences in *use, meaning* and *register*, where appropriate, between a word and its synonym, Asking students to write sentences exemplifying each synonym will help in the process of widening their productive vocabulary.
>
> You can point out, for example, that **distressed, faculty, acquisition** and **corroborative** are all more formal than their synonyms. **Regressing** in this context is transitive, but **reverting** is intransitive. And the meaning of **perpetuate** is more limited and specific than that of **preserve**.

TASK 10

10.1 Before you begin this exercise, it may help to elicit the differences between *relative* and *absolute*, and why these terms are opposed in meaning. Otherwise some students may have trouble distinguishing between *relative* and *flexible*, for example.

Attitude	Stage of development
(b) Experts know everything.	1 (and to some extent 2)
(c) Theories are flexible.	2
(d) Theories are relative.	3
(e) Learning means remembering facts.	1
(f) There are no absolute truths.	3 (and to some extent 2)
(g) Independence of thought is a desirable goal.	3
(h) Valid experimental results are widely generalisable.	1/2*
(i) Theories can be applied universally.	2
(j) All individuals can evaluate facts or theories.	3

*The scope of the reference item **This** in line 39 is not entirely clear. It is taken to include lines 33–8 (**He noted** ...), but it could extend as far back as line 29 (**but they also over-generalised** ...). For this reason the answer for attitude (h) is given as either 1 or 2. This may be a good opportunity to point out that academic texts are not always as well-written as our teaching suggests.

If students still seem to have difficulty in understanding some of the concepts in this text, you can summarise the differences between Perry's second and third stages as follows:

Stage 2 = Theories are seen as generalised; they are flexible and can be altered or reshaped in any way; they are often a matter of opinion; they can be applied in all circumstances (universally).

Stage 3 = Theories are seen as clearly defined and specific; they are relative to particular times and conditions; they need to be evaluated by individuals; they cannot be applied universally.

Task 11

11.1 Yes. It is worth pointing out that the conduct of the argument is formal and impersonal and gives the impression of relative neutrality. The writer's attitudes, however, are revealed in two ways:

(a) The ironic use of inverted commas in lines, 5, 24, 25, 42 and 44.

(b) The final sentence in the text, lines 53–7, reveals the writer's attitude in the conclusions that are drawn. **Obviously** at the opening of the sentence provides a clear and emphatic marker.

Task 12

12.1 Formal and impersonal. The term *register* could be introduced and explained here (i.e. style of language and specific items of language chosen for their suitability for a given readership, audience, purpose or situation).

Specific features:

(a) Formal, academic choice of vocabulary. It would help to elicit and list some of these on the board/OHP: **critical faculty** (line 14), **quantitative data** (line 31), **regressing** (line 31), **corroborative observation** (lines 33–4), etc.

(b) Long, complex sentence structures. These are a characteristic feature of formal, academic writing. See especially lines 26–33, 44–9, etc.

(c) The absence of contracted verb forms.

(d) The avoidance of any first-person reference (*I, we*).

12.2 Readers with academic interests in education, psychology, sociology, etc.

12.3 An academic book or journal would be the most likely source for this.

Preparation for Writing Unit 1

If you are using the Writing book in this series, it would help to emphasise that the two texts in this unit are examples of academic writing. Refer again to the examples of sources and references given in Task 8.

If students still seem not to have a full understanding of what academic writing means, it would help to show them one or two other examples and contrast these with selections from non-academic texts (popular magazines/newspapers, letters, etc.). In Writing Unit 1, they will be asked to give their views about academic writing.

TASK 13

13.1–3 The discussion questions should bring out some interesting cultural differences on this topic, especially if the group is heterogeneous in its composition.

The texts in this unit embody specifically Western assumptions about individual responsibility and learner independence which may not be relevant to the economic and cultural conditions of some countries. Some students, in discussing these questions, have said that their own learning cultures are more authoritarian or conservative than those in the West, and that the third stage of intellectual development as outlined by Perry would not be acceptable in these conditions.

TASK 14

14.1 Students can be given a relatively free hand with this essay topic. You may want to devise a related topic more suitable for the interests of your group. You may also want students to read or find other texts relating to those in this unit.

It may help to introduce some of the conventions of referring to sources at this point, so that students can incorporate references to the reading texts in this unit or to other texts. (See the Study Skills volume in this series.)

UNIT 2
COUNSELLING OVERSEAS STUDENTS

It may be helpful to elicit the meaning of the term *counselling* at the outset. A simple definition is: the act of giving professional advice about problems. In this context, the problems can be both personal and academic. Counselling in this sense will be unfamiliar to students from some cultures.

PRE-READING TASKS

A. Students may misinterpret the title as introducing a text about language learning, despite the explanations given. It would be best to check their comprehension of the title and the description of the topic before they begin formulating their questions. Emphasise that the questions should be written down so that they can refer to them again in Task 15.

 Text 2.1

TASK 1

1.1 It may be best to announce a specific time limit before students begin to skim. This can vary according to the needs and proficiency level of the group.

1.2 Try to elicit the overall idea before they carry out a second reading in Task 2.1; i.e. the problems of applying Western forms of counselling to overseas students.

TASK 2

2.1 You may want to elicit the students' understanding of the main ideas before they go on to do this exercise, especially if they find the text difficult.

2.2   (a) 5   (b) 1   (c) 4   (d) 2   (e) 3

Task 3

3.1 Corrected versions of false statements are variable. Those given below are only suggestions.

   (a) **F.** The problems experienced by overseas students are caused by many factors: differences in climate and culture as well as academic and language difficulties.

   (b) **F.** University counsellors and doctors often fail to deal with these problems effectively because their psychological theories are ethnocentric or based on Western models.

   (c) **T** if 'many' is considered close enough to **several** in the text, **F** if not (line 18). This may be a good opportunity to highlight the differences between *most, many, a number of, several, few*, etc.
   'A number of years' would be more accurate.

   (d) **F.** The statement is too unqualified. It would be more accurate to say that this terminology can further confuse, or often further confuses, an overseas student who is already experiencing such problems. You may want to refer again to work on qualification done in Unit 1, Task 4.

   (e) **F.** Mr Coren does not agree that Western psychological theories are likely to help many overseas students.

   (f) **T.** (lines 27–31).

Task 4

4.1   1. (b)   2. (c)   3. (a)   4. (c)   5. (a)

4.2   1. psychosomatic   3. estranged   5. deteriorating
         2. perplex   4. nationalist

Again, it would be useful to elicit the students' understanding of *synonym* and *antonym* before doing this exercise.

Once they have matched each word with its appropriate synonym, you may want to go on to explain the slight differences in use and meaning between these synonymous pairs. You could also emphasise that they should be alert to such differences between synonyms in a language which contains an often bewildering range and variety for a non-native speaker.

> Students can also be advised to invest in a thesaurus for vocabulary-building. It is important to emphasise, however, that they should choose one specifically designed for learners of English as a second language. In other words, they should look for one which contains examples of usage to clarify the differences between synonyms for non-native speakers. You may want to recommend specific titles such as:
>
> – *Longman Language Activator (A Production Dictionary)*
> – *Roget's Thesaurus of English Words and Phrases*
>   (published by Penguin and Longman)
> – *Chambers Thesaurus*
> – *The Collins Thesaurus*
> – *The Oxford Thesaurus*

TASK 5

5.1 Paragraph 4, lines 17–24.

5.2 Emphasise that students should avoid repeating the language of the text as much as possible.

5.3 (a) Mr Coren is a psychotherapist in a reputable academic institution.
(b) He has practised for a number of years, especially with overseas students.

5.4 (a) Psychological explanations can be found for physical ailments (lines 14–16).
(b) The importance of the behaviour of individuals, as distinct from groups (lines 19–24).
(c) The freedom to choose and change academic courses is desirable (lines 27–31).

TASK 6

The exercises in Task 6 focus on *degree of certainty*. You may want to emphasise that assessing the degree of certainty expressed in a writer's arguments is very important in reading academic texts. It is also important when students introduce and qualify generalisations in their own academic writing. Refer them again to the work already done on this in Unit 1, Task 4. Degree of certainty is taken up again in Unit 7.

6.1 Line 18: **believes**. There is a moderately high degree of certainty expressed in this verb. In other words, the speaker about to be quoted seems reasonably confident about the validity of his views. The question of evidence to support these views, however, is largely anecdotal in what follows.

6.2 Synonyms can be elicited and ranked in order of the certainty which they express or imply. For example:

1. proves	6. defends	11. feels
2. demonstrates	7. agrees/disagrees	12. suggests
3. shows	8. claims	13. supposes
4. insists	9. thinks	
5. asserts	10. considers	

You may also want to ask students to place 'believes' in the appropriate place on this scale. It is approximately equivalent to 'asserts', or can be placed between 'asserts' and 'insists'.

6.3 The word **unlikely** makes it clear that Mr Coren does not feel this argument is always or universally valid. Again, he can be described as asserting his views with a moderately high degree of certainty. Refer students back to the work done in Unit 1, Task 4, involving qualification in terms of probability.

Synonyms for **unlikely** are 'improbable', 'doubtful', 'not expected'. These synonyms could not replace **unlikely** in the sentence as it stands, however.

6.4 Some other words expressing probability, in decreasing order of degree:

certainly	maybe
undoubtedly	uncertain
probable/probably	doubtful
likely	unlikely
conceivably	improbable
possible/possibly	impossible
perhaps	

You may want to caution students that these words have different uses in different contexts and are not necessarily interchangeable in the same structure. It would help to elicit or give some examples of actual use in sentences and to write them on the board/OHP.

TASK 7

7.1 (What the writer imagines to be) a typical overseas student whose experience illustrates most of the characteristic problems encountered.

7.2
- The article opens with a direct and apparently personal account of a typical individual's experience.
- It creates a dramatic opening designed to capture the reader's attention and stimulate curiosity about the background and solutions to these problems.

- The concrete examples and implied narrative provide a useful counter-balance to the more generalised and theoretical discussion which follows.

You may want to postpone pointing out that these are often features of effective journalistic writing as distinct from academic writing. This is covered in Task 13.

Text 2.2

TASK 8

8.1   (a) **a gathering of university and polytechnic student counsellors** (lines 43–4) *or* **the annual conference of the Association of Student Counsellors** (lines 52–3). Either of these answers is acceptable.

(b) North America (line 56) and the Middle East (line 60).

TASK 9

9.2 Encourage students to express the main ideas in their own words, as much as possible. After a second reading they should be able to describe most of the important ides.

TASK 10

10.1   1. (b)   2. (a)   3. (b)   4. (c)   5. (c)

10.2   1. personality
2. independence
3. aggravation
4. dialect (there are important differences here, however)
5. go-between

It would be useful to point out the differences in formality between **make-up/personality** and **intermediary/go-between**.

This may be a good opportunity to remind students of the terms *immediate context* and *wider context* which they have seen in the chapter 'Introducing this book' and which you probably referred to in the vocabulary exercise in Unit 1. The answer to 5, in particular, would require looking at the wider context to guess the meaning of **intermediary**.

TASK 11

11.1 Counsellors should first attempt to study and understand the student's culture before deciding how to approach his/her problems.

11.2 After he had failed to treat several 'cases' effectively with a Western psychological approach.

TASK 12

12.1 **must** (line 50). He is asserting a high degree of certainty here. Contrast **unlikely** (line 20) in Text 2.1, paragraph 4.

12.2 **should perhaps** (line 70) signals a more cautious and qualified conclusion. It is interesting that these words express less certainty than others he has used.

TASK 13

> The important point to be made here is that these texts are not examples of academic writing. They are characteristic of the 'quality' journalism found in *The Times Higher Education Supplement* and similar publications, and provide useful contrasts in terms of style and content with other, more specifically academic reading texts in this book.
>
> You may want to compare these texts in detail with those in Unit 1 so that students have a clear sense of the distinctions between academic and other forms of writing. The texts in this unit contain many features of formal, academic writing, and the subject matter is academic. Nevertheless, many of the distinguishing features of journalism are clear. Contrast, for example, the much longer, more complex sentence structures in the texts in Unit 1 with the shorter, simpler sentence structures and paragraphs here.
>
> Refer students again to the work done on features of style and language use in Unit 1, Task 12.

13.1 The writer's use of language is relatively formal but contains a number of less formal or informal elements. The style is on the whole impersonal, but there are personal elements in the passages in which Alex Coren is quoted (e.g. Text 2.1, line 22: **we … our**).

These texts are not examples of academic writing, but they contain a number of features of formal, academic style. The dramatic narrative which opens Text 2.1

makes it clear that this is not academic writing. So do the passages in which the writer quotes Mr Coren's spoken words. Features of informal style include **just do not believe in the assumptions** (Text 2.1, lines 25–6), and the less formal vocabulary item **make-up** (Text 2.2, line 34).

13.2 Relatively educated readers with interests in education, psychology, sociology, anthropology or cultural studies.

13.3 The most likely forms of publication would be in a 'quality' newspaper or supplement or in periodicals written for a similar readership, such as *The Economist.*

TASK 14

14.1 The title is deliberately brief and suggestive, in its use of a well-worn phrase, rather than explanatory. It prepares the reader for a probable situation in which one person or group needs to find a way to communicate effectively with another, but it gives no specific information about the situation or context.

14.2 Ask the students to compose sub-titles which:

(a) provide enough specific information to complement the main title
(b) do not repeat the terms of the main title
(c) are written in an appropriate style for a 'quality' newspaper or supplement
(d) are clear and interesting for potential readers.

After pair work in which they apply these criteria, their answers can be put on the board and opinions elicited about which are the most effective, and why. This exercise can produce some interesting results and animated discussion.

The original sub-title was: 'Western-style counselling can risk bewildering alienated overseas students'. Anything similar is acceptable. Some students may even improve on this.

TASK 15

15.1 At this point it may be useful to elicit what students think about the purpose and value of asking and answering predicting questions before reading texts, even if the results are not entirely accurate. You can remind them that this has been proven through research to be an effective reading strategy. By assessing their expectations of a text before they read, they can achieve a more concentrated focus and improve their comprehension.

Remind them that the object of predicting exercises is not to get the 'right answers'.

TASK 16

16.1–3 The discussion on these topics can be very interesting. Many students come from cultures in which Western-style counselling has little or no influence. Even if it is available, traditional social patterns are often still operating – i.e. a person will go to an elder, to a religious leader, to a close friend of the parents, to a grandparent, etc., to discuss serious problems. It is ironic that the need for and continuing growth of Western psychological counselling also testify to the disintegration of these traditional networks in Western societies.

TASK 17

17.1 Students can be given a relatively free hand with this essay topic. You may want to devise a related topic more suitable for the interests of your group. Other possibilities are to provide them with further texts of your own choice or to ask them to find at least one additional text which can be used as source material for the essay.

It may help to introduce some of the conventions of referring to sources at this point, so that students can incorporate references to the reading texts in this unit or from other texts. (See the Study Skills volume in this series.)

UNIT 3

URBAN DEVELOPMENT

PRE-READING TASKS

A. After initial discussion, students can be referred to Figure 3.1 to ascertain the answers to each question.

   (a) According to Figure 3.1, the largest city is Tokyo, followed by New York and Mexico City.
   (b) The fastest-growing city is Bandung, followed by Lagos and Karachi. Bogotá and Baghdad vie for fourth position.

To interpret Figure 3.1 students may need to use a ruler. Otherwise the vertical indicators of growth rate can be difficult to measure.

B. Problems associated with large, overcrowded cities can include pollution of air, water and the urban environment; high unemployment; homelessness; crime; and inadequate or overcrowded transport.

 Text 3.1

TASK 1

1.2 Problems mentioned in the text include inadequate housing; lack of mains drainage and water supply; lack of services such as refuse disposal; unemployment and under-employment; and starving children (lines 17–27).

TASK 2

2.1   (a) The city which grew the least appears to be Moscow, although this is not quite clear. Some students may say London. Either is acceptable. Paris is a close third.

(b) Calcutta
(c) Lima

The purpose of (b) and (c) is to underline the difference between size and growth rate. You may want to pose some additional questions if students still have difficulty interpreting the information in the figure.

TASK 3

3.2 The proportion of people living in towns is much greater than the proportion of people working in industry (lines 11–16). The consequent inability of cities to pay for their growth is also relevant (lines 17–19).

> Although there is no vocabulary exercise for Text 3.1, you may want to elicit the students' understanding of words such as **alarming** (line 3), **sheer** (line 7), **urban** (line 22), **despairing** (line 25) and **undeterred** (line 27).

TASK 4

Before you address this question, you may want to elicit the students' understanding of *infer*: to understand something which is implied or expressed indirectly. You may want to give examples of ways in which writers can assume knowledge on the part of their readers and of how this knowledge can often be specific to a culture or an intellectual discipline.

It would also be helpful to establish clearly the formal semantic distinctions between *infer* and *imply*, which are sometimes not observed in informal contexts.

4.1 Both groups were industrialising. This can be inferred from lines 9–16. Some students may have trouble making this inference, however.

TASK 5

5.1 **as you can see in Figure 3.1** (line 3)   **As you can see from Table 3.1** (line 11)

It would be worth pointing out that these forms of words are less formal than those in 5.2 below because of the use of **you**.

5.2 Examples include:

As can be seen in …
It can be seen from …

It is apparent/clear from …
According to …
As (is) shown in …

You may want to ask students to write sentences in which these phrases are used. It would also be a good idea to check the students' understanding of the following forms in which data can be represented visually: charts, pie diagrams/charts, diagrams, tables and graphs.

> Before starting Text 3.2, you may want to elicit the students' knowledge of the Industrial Revolution and where and approximately when it started. The text may present material which is unfamiliar to some students.

 # Text 3.2 and Text 3.3

TASK 6

> It would help to elicit students' understanding of the term *capital* before you ask them to consider the title. A simple definition is: money or property that can be used to produce more wealth.

6.1 No. 'As if' followed by 'only' or 'merely' usually introduces a fallacy. This is another example of the need to infer a writer's meaning.

   You can then pose the further question: 'What else would the writer consider to be important?' The appropriate answer would be 'people' or 'human beings'.

6.2 See especially line 15 (**pushed off**), line 19 (**bleak**) and line 21 (**private greed**), in which clear value judgements are expressed. These confirm the expectations created by the title.

TASK 7

7.2   (a) the population
      (b) villages to cities
      (c) cities than in villages
      (d) very bad

Similar answers are acceptable. Students can be asked in each case to cite a specific sentence in the text to support their answers.

TASK 8

8.1   1. (c)   2. (a)   3. (b)   4. (b)   5. (a)   6. (c)

8.2
1. largely
2. birthplace
3. dismal
4. avarice
5. randomly
6. disastrous

> In Task 8 and in other vocabulary exercises involving synonyms and antonyms in this book, it is suggested that you take time to explain some of the differences in use, meaning and register, where appropriate, between a word and its synonym.
>
> You can point out, for example, that **avarice** is considerably more formal or academic than **greed** in 4. Asking students to write sentences exemplifying each synonym will help in the process of widening their productive vocabulary.

TASK 9

9.1
    (b) **human and animal power** (line 4)
    (c) **power based on coal and steam** (lines 11–12)
    (d) **industrial towns, cities and ports** (lines 16–17)
    (e) **rural** (line 18)
    (f) **cities** (line 20)
    (g) **broader social values, community concerns and human dignity** (line 22)

It would help to elicit the students' understanding of the phrases in (g), once they have identified the contrast. These can be described more simply as involving a moral concern for the welfare of all individuals in a society.

TASK 10

10.1 Three, although the second and third overlap.

10.2
  ● **In the early part of the eighteenth century** (line 1)
    ● **From the late eighteenth and throughout the nineteenth centuries** (lines 13–14)
    ● **By the middle of the nineteenth century** (line 17)

It would be helpful to elicit and explain here the different uses and implications of the prepositions *in, from, throughout* and *by* in expressions involving time. It would also be a useful exercise for students to assign specific numerical dates to these periods so that the conventions of referring to centuries in English are clear to them. Approximate dates would be:

- 1700–1740
- 1770–1899
- (1770)–1850

The third time period contains implicit reference to the second and continues to develop the topic of rural–urban migration.

You may want to expand on the point that chronological order is widely used, especially in narrative texts, but other ways of organising references to time are also commonly found in academic writing.

10.3 They are part of the basis of the text organisation. The two paragraphs contrast pre-Industrial Revolution conditions with those after it had begun (cf. Unit 1, Task 2). There is a 'vertical' pattern of contrast here, but this point can be postponed until Task 16.

> It may be helpful to elicit a definition of *capitalism* before you start Text 3.3:
>
> **capitalism**: a system of production and trade based on the private ownership of wealth, free buying and selling, and little industrial activity by the government.
>
> (*Longman Dictionary of Contemporary English*)

TASK 11

11.1 (c) The control of capitalism

11.2 Skimming, evaluating titles and (to some extent) identifying main ideas.

If students have difficulty with this, refer them to the chapter 'Introducing this book' to review the terminology. See also the statement of aims which opens this unit.

> It is recommended that from time to time you check students' understanding of the reading skills and strategies which they have practised in individual tasks. This will promote a more conscious awareness of their reading and the gradual development of fluency in the appropriate metalanguage.

TASK 12

12.2 To support their final choice of a sub-title after a second reading, students can be asked to identify topic sentences in each paragraph, especially if they are still uncertain about their choice.

Refer them especially to **The rise of capitalist industrialism** (lines 32–5) and **limits on capitalist forms of development** (line 49). On this basis students should be able to choose (c) more clearly.

TASK 13

13.1
1. (a) – cf. **virtues, efficiency** (lines 33, 34)
2. (b) – cf. **by price** (line 39)
3. (b) – cf. **a belief** (line 41)
4. (c) – cf. line 43 and **taken up by** (lines 46–7)
5. (a) – cf. **worst excesses** (line 53)

The context provides clues to the meanings of words, as indicated. 2 and 4 would also benefit from a study of the wider context.

13.2
1. glorified	3. religion	5. unrestrained
2. worth	4. propounded	

> Before Task 14, it may be useful to elicit some of the common cohesive words and phrases and list them on the board/OHP under headings such as:
>
> | **Addition** | **Contrast** | **Alternative** | **Relative** |
> |---|---|---|---|
> | and | but | or | which |
>
> See also Unit 5, Task 12. If you are using the Writing book in this series, see the appendices for lists of cohesive markers.

TASK 14

14.1
which (lines 33, 39, 41)	**also** (line 50)
and (lines 36, 52, etc.)	**where** (line 50)
In time (line 38)	**eventually** (line 53)
(not ...) but (lines 39–40)	**that** (line 54)
To be sure (line 43)	**but** (line 56)

There are many examples of *and* in Text 3.3 operating at phrase level. Advise the students to look only for connectives and cohesive phrases linking clauses or major parts of sentences.

14.2 **In time** (line 38); **Eventually** (line 53)

14.3 **(not ...) but** (lines 39–40); **but** (line 56)

> You may also want to focus specifically on the cohesive function of relative words and structures here:
>
> **which** (lines 33, 41) **where** (line 50)
> **in which** (line 39) **that** (line 54)
>
> It would be useful to stress the importance of relative structures in academic writing generally. Less proficient students tend to have problems with these in their writing, and do not use enough of them.

TASK 15

15.1 Once the students have ascertained that a specific attitude or bias is revealed, ask them to identify one sentence which most clearly expresses this. Appropriate choices would be:

In time ... good for all. (lines 38–42)
The industrial cities ... rampant capitalism. (lines 49–53)

Lines 56–7 are also possible but contain less information.

> You may want to highlight other features that express or imply the writer's attitude through value judgements in the text:
>
> 1. the use of inverted commas with **perfect** (line 40) and **natural** (line 41)
> 2. **a cog in the machine of production** to describe the exploitation of human beings (lines 36–7)
> 3. the collocation **competitive, selfish** (line 42)
> 4. **the worst excesses of a rampant capitalism** (line 53; abridged in line 56).
>
> It would help to emphasise to students that these skills in identifying and analysing a writer's attitude will be very important in their degree courses, especially when they are asked to write critically about their reading in their academic subject.

TASK 16

16.1 This paragraph should provide a very simplified introduction to a pattern of organisation which many students find difficult either to recognise or produce. It follows a 'vertical' pattern. This pattern can be elicited and illustrated on the board as follows:

16.2 Remind students before they begin this exercise that rewriting the paragraph in a 'horizontal' pattern will involve a greater use of markers of contrast. The following is one of a number of possible examples:

> Apples are generally oval in shape, whereas most oranges are more round. Apples range in colour from green to yellow to red, but the colour range of oranges is more limited – from vermillion to pale orange. Apples are usually firm in texture, sometimes even hard, while oranges are relatively soft.

16.3 Both Texts 3.2 and 3.3 follow a loosely 'vertical' pattern of contrast. It is more easily recognisable in Text 3.2 than in 3.3. In both of these texts, however, the order of points in the first and second paragraphs does not closely correspond.

The completion of Task 10 should also enable students to answer this question in relation to Text 3.2 more easily.

It could be pointed out that the last sentence in the second paragraph of Text 3.3 presents a further contrast (**but the market system** ...) which refers back to the previous paragraph and has a unifying effect.

> It would help to emphasise that these 'horizontal' and 'vertical' patterns of comparison and contrast are not always used as methodically by writers as the diagrams or this simplified paragraph suggest. Nor do writers necessarily make consistent use of the appropriate markers. These factors can complicate the recognition of this rhetorical function for non-native speakers.
>
> These patterns are also considered in Unit 3 of the Writing book in this series.

TASK 17

17.1 Answers could include parks, libraries, community centres, leisure centres and sports facilities or clubs.

17.2 Answers will vary widely. Emphasise that students should focus on a specific city which they have lived in or visited, in contrast to the more generalised discussion earlier in this unit.

Task 18

18.1 You may want to devise a related topic more suitable for the interests of your group. Other possibilities are to provide them with further texts of your own choice or to ask them to find at least one additional text which can be used as source material for the essay.

Students can be asked to organise their essay according to a 'vertical' or 'horizontal' pattern of comparison/contrast. If you are using the Writing book in this series, however, students can organise their essay more freely if you wish. They will be asked to follow one of these patterns of organisation in the essay for Writing Unit 3.

UNIT 4

GLOBAL WARMING

 Text 4.1

TASK 1

1.1 It might be guessed that carbon 'goes in' and 'comes out', and that the two amounts are not equal. Similar answers are acceptable. You may want to introduce the term *metaphor* to describe the figurative use of **budget** in the title.

1.2 Carbon 'goes out' of the biosphere (expenditure) and 'comes into' the atmosphere (income), and vice-versa. In this way there is a 'budget'. In 1986 the amounts held by each were 563 gigatonnes and 730 gigatonnes, respectively.

TASK 2

2.1 (a) 'Causes of increasing atmospheric carbon' is a more accurate summary of lines 6–35. The text does *not* suggest any measures to redress the balance.

As a further exercise, students could be asked to expand this title to make it more specific and inclusive, e.g. 'Causes of increasing atmospheric carbon and scientific uncertainty about its effects'.

TASK 3

3.2

> 1986 carbon in atmosphere = 730 gigatonnes
>   carbon in biosphere   = 563 gigatonnes
>
> Increase of carbon in atmosphere since pre-industrial times = 155 gigatonnes
>
> Causes of increase in atmospheric carbon = (a) burning fossil fuels
>   (b) destruction of vegetation

Effects on temperature = a rise of between 1.5 and 5.5 degrees Celsius in the late 21st century.

Other locations of carbon = (a) oceans
(b) soils

TASK 4

4.1   1. (c)   2. (a)   3. (b)   4. (a)   5. (b)   6. (c)

4.2   1. absorb   3. dribble   5. foods
          2. cycle (this is not a close   4. unsteady   6. discharges
             synonym, however)

> This would be a good opportunity to point out some of the stylistic diversity often found in journals of this kind, which are written for both a specialist and a more general readership. Their style can sometimes confuse students because it exhibits broadly formal features but often contains a number of less formal or informal elements. **Turnover** and **shaky** are less formal than the other vocabulary items here and would not be acceptable in many forms of academic writing. You may also want to refer students back to the work done on language use in Unit 2, in which the texts came from another quality journal.
>
> The mixture of formal and informal elements is more pronounced in Text 4.2, and for this reason it would help to alert students to it here. See also Task 11 in this unit.
>
> You may also want to emphasise that this text is not academic writing in the strict sense, although it is very close to it in many of its features. Point out that although students will not need to write like this themselves, much of the material they will read for general information (professional and specialist magazines, popularised academic writing, good quality journalism) will display such features.

TASK 5

5.1 The formal definition is found in lines 1–2 of the text. It is extended in lines 2–5. Its three components are:

1. **photosynthesis**
2. **process**
3. **cycles carbon between the atmosphere and the biosphere**

This would be a good opportunity to show students an example of the naming definition:

       (2)   **(3)**
The process that cycles carbon between the atmosphere and the biosphere is
                             (1)
called/termed/named photosynthisis.

Instead of showing this example initially, you may want to give the students the task of writing the definition in another way, using the same elements in another order:

2. **process**
3. **cycles carbon between the atmosphere and the biosphere**
1. **photosynthesis**

They can work in pairs on this and try to connect the three elements in an appropriate way.

> Students can be given more practice in defining terms in either of these ways, if you feel they need it. You can choose terms which would be most familiar to the students through their subject areas.

TASK 6

6.1 These measurements have not been proven by scientific research. See especially lines 21–7 and 32–3.

6.2 It is recommended that you check whether students understand the distinction between *tentative* (degree of certainty) and *approximate* (degree of exactness) before you ask them to do this exercise. Ask them to identify specific words in each answer which relate to these concepts; for example:

> **current estimates** (approximate) **suggest** (tentative)
>
> **an estimated 730 Gt** (line 4)
> **Current estimates suggest** (line 6)
> **relatively small** (lines 12, 17)
> **an estimated 2.2 Gt a year** (line 13)
> **about 155 Gt** (line 16)
> **between 1.5 and 5.5 degrees Celsius** (line 19)
> **estimated to hold** (line 23–4)
> **Estimates suggest** (line 30)

You may also want to include the tentative use of **could** (line 18) and give examples of similar uses of modal verbs.

6.3 They make clear the limited and uncertain nature of scientific knowledge on this subject.

You may also want to refer to a series of noun phrases used in the text to emphasise the limited data available:

lack of precision (line 21)
very shaky knowledge (line 22)
no detailed information (line 24)
little idea (line 32)

TASK 7

7.1 The writer's purpose is primarily to inform. The article does, however, contain some attempt to persuade. The writer advocates a particular point of view about the nature and extent of scientific knowledge on this subject. This is made most explicit in lines 21–7 and·32–3.

This may be a good opportunity to emphasise that writers are rarely 'neutral', even in texts primarily designed to inform. Compare Unit 3, Task 15.

 # Text 4.2 and Text 4.3

TASK 8

8.2 The writer proposes (b), limited action. See especially lines 66–74 in Text 4.3. If students have trouble digesting an article of this length, ask them to read it (both texts) a second time and then discuss their ideas with a partner before they choose one of the three alternatives in this task. You can also divide Text 4.2 into more digestible sections for skimming, if you prefer.

TASK 9

9.2   (a) 6   (b) 7   (c) 4   (d) 1   (e) 2   (f) 8   (g) 5   (h) 3

TASK 10

10.1   1.(b)   2. (a)   3. (c)   4. (c)   5. (a)   6. (b)   7. (b)   8. (c)

10.2 1. interwoven   4. impetus   7. caution
          2. flow   5. disturbances   8. avoid
          3. stylish   6. incentive

As suggested before, it would be a good idea to focus on differences of meaning, register or use between these words and their synonyms. Illustrations of use in sentences on the board/OHP would also help.

TASK 11

11.1 The writer's use of language is relatively formal and impersonal, but it contains many informal vocabulary items and expressions (see 11.2). Some of the sentences are unusually long and complex and may present difficulties for some students. See especially lines 58–60 and 71–4. Remind students of the style of quality journals discussed in Task 4.

11.2 The following words and phrases are less formal or informal in their register:

(a) a much better **trapper** of heat (line 13)
(b) and **what-have-you** (line 18)
(c) a **teetering** balance (line 37)
(d) once **triggered** (line 45)
(e) **to ride out** such ... upheavals (line 55)
(f) the ozone-**chomping** CFCs (line 61)
(g) in **a piecemeal sort of way** (line 67)
(h) **have a shot at** global air-conditioning (line 69)
(i) forever **jiggling** them (line 73)
(j) **to play at** planet management (line 80)

It would be useful to ascertain the students' understanding of each of these items and explain them as necessary. It would also help to emphasise that these words and phrases, while they contribute an element of 'colour' and interest to the style of the article, would not be acceptable in many forms of academic writing.

TASK 12

12.1 Paragraph 5 (lines 44–56) contrasts with paragraph 6 (lines 57–65) in at least two ways:

1. past/present
2. climate change can be radical/it may never happen

The writer presents a balance of views which are sustained in some tension with each other. They can be described as *complementary* rather than inconsistent.

(Remind students of the differences between *complementary* and *complimentary*.) You may want to give the following definition:

> **complementary**: *adj.* making something complete; supplying what is lacking or needed for completion.
>
> *(Longman Dictionary of Contemporary English)*

Some students may find this form of thinking difficult to grasp initially, however. If so, some further examples of complementary truths/observations from their own subject areas may help.

12.2 The writer reminds the reader that **The climate changes constantly** in line 71. This was also the emphasis in the opening paragraph.

The purpose of this is to unify the text so that to some extent it ends as it began. You may want to point out that this is often a feature of effective conclusions in academic writing.

TASK 13

13.1 Texts 4.2 and 4.3 broadly follow this pattern of organisation, which can be outlined as follows:

	Paragraphs
SITUATION	1
PROBLEM	2–4
SOLUTION	5 and 6
EVALUATION	7 and 8

The third paragraph distinguishes between the greenhouse effect and global warming and questions the nature and effect of the problem. Its concerns are still with the problem, however.

TASK 14

14.1 Examples of extended definition are:

> Global warming is a process in which increasing amounts of carbon dioxide, CFCs, methane and other gases trap heat in the earth's atmosphere and cause a gradual rise in the earth's temperature.

> Global warming may be defined as a process by means of which increasing amounts of carbon dioxide, CFCs, methane and other gases trap heat in the earth's atmosphere. This causes a gradual rise in the earth's temperature.

Similar answers are acceptable, as long as they include all of the items of information given and are linked coherently.

TASK 15

15.3 To stimulate discussion and provide more subject input for the essay, you may want to refer the students to other sources of information in a library. You may also want to distribute other texts of your own on global warming or related issues.

TASK 16

16.1–3 The discussion questions may reveal some interesting differences of opinion on these issues. Some may feel that environmental issues are not important, particularly if the effects of some problems, such as global warming, will not be felt during the present generation. Others may feel that they are considerably less important than the need for economic development, especially in developing countries.

TASK 17

17.1 You may want to devise related topics more suitable for the interests of your group. You may also want students to read or find other texts relating to those in this unit.

If students seem able and willing to produce the **Situation→Problem→Solution→Evaluation** pattern in their writing at this point, they can be encouraged to use it in their essays and to plan their writing accordingly. Some may feel that they would like to organise the essay in a different way, however. More specific practice in using this pattern of organisation is given in Units 4 and 6 of the Writing book in this series, and it would be best to avoid the impression of repetition if you are using this.

You can also emphasise the structures of *definition* and *extended definition*. Students can be asked to define key terms such as 'economic development', 'developed/developing countries' or 'global warming'. You may also want to give them more latitude in their approach to either topic, especially if you are using the Writing book in this series.

UNIT 5

EDUCATION IN ASIA

 Text 5.1

TASK 1

1.1 The sub-title 'Types of education' should help students here. The writer discusses and defines development in the first paragraph and in the following paragraphs outlines the four major forms of education, which can contribute to development:

1. Formal education or schooling
2. Informal education
3. Nonformal education
4. Education for self-reliance and participation.

TASK 2

2.2 Development can be defined as either:

(a) economic growth, which tends to benefit those with higher incomes, or
(b) improving the standard of living of the poorest 40 per cent of the population.

The writer sees formal education as contributing to development in the first sense (lines 3–5) but failing to foster development in the second sense (lines 7–8).

2.3 According to the writer, this is caused by mechanisms such as regressive tax systems, expensive secondary schooling and free higher education, which tend to benefit families already on high incomes (lines 11–13).

2.4 Lines 13–15: **For this article I will define development …**

2.5 The writer extends this definition by adding that development of this kind needs:

(a) political systems more responsive to the needs of the poor (lines 15–17)

(b) rising real income as well as more equal distribution and management of wealth (lines 17–18).

2.6 The definition is expressed and structured in less formal terms than those found in Unit 4, Task 5 and 14. The writer also uses the first person reference *I*.
Nevertheless it contains the three basic components of formal definition:

1. Name of the term being defined (**development**)
2. Class to which it belongs (**movement**)
3. Special features ([**which attempts to create**] **a more humane society**).

You may want to ask students how this could be rewritten as a more formal definition. For example:

Development can be defined as a programme of action which attempts to create a more humane society in both developed and developing countries.

See Task 15, where points of style are taken up more fully.

TASK 3

3.1 Four forms of education are outlined in Text 5.1:

1. **Formal education or schooling** (lines 20–2)
2. **Informal education** (lines 22–32)
3. **Nonformal education** (lines 33–9)
4. **Education for self-reliance and participation** (lines 40–64)

You may want to add that the considerably greater development given by the writer to the last form of education reveals the emphasis in the paragraphs that will follow Text 5.1. Clearly the writer believes that this form of education is most essential for development as he defines it in lines 13–15.

3.2 Formal education (lines 20–2) is not illustrated by examples. This and the unusually brief development given to this form of education reflect the dominant interests of the writer in relation to his topic.

3.3 Education for self-reliance and participation, according to Julius Nyerere in lines 59–62.

3.4 Nyerere uses a contrast between active and passive verb forms to emphasise his point, and this contrast is then echoed by the writer:

(a) **People can only develop themselves; they cannot be developed.**

(b) **The rural poor have to transform themselves from being acted upon to being actors.**

In each case the emphasis is on people empowering themselves from within the terms of their own societies and cultures.

Task 4

4.1 Something similar to the following would be acceptable:

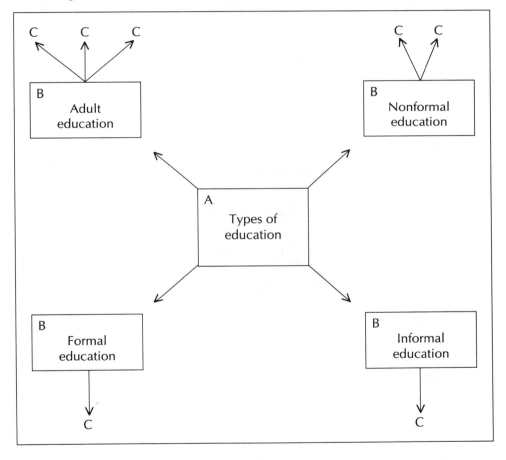

Students can go on to provide some of the supporting information and examples in note form in the places indicated by a 'C'.

You may also want to illustrate other forms of mind maps, such as those using circles and connecting arrows or curves.

Mind mapping, as is indicated in the Student's Book, can be a helpful strategy for understanding the structure of main ideas in a reading text. You may want to practise this in relation to other reading texts, such as those in Units 6 and 7 or others you may have in mind. Some students also find mind maps useful when they plan their essays.

TASK 5

5.1 1. (b) 2. (a) 3. (c) 4. (c) 5. (b) 6. (a)

5.2 1. successful people 3. reduction 5. democratic
2. callous 4. results 6. intertia

TASK 6

6.1 (a) [the widening of] the gap between rich and poor (lines 9–10)
(b) the People's Republic of China (line 27)
(c) nonformal education and formal education (lines 36–7)
(d) adult education for self-reliance and participation (line 40)
(e) adult education for self-reliance and participation (line 40). There is another, intermediate reference item here also: the approach in line 45.
(f) the often paternalistic community development approach of the past (lines 50–1)
(g) groups of people (line 47) is what it ultimately refers to. There are other, intermediate reference items as well here: They (line 48) and These adult groups (line 51–2).

Examples (e) and (g) provide useful opportunities to illustrate the potential complexity of the use of reference items in reading texts and the necessity for students to keep them clear in their minds as they read.

You may want to point out the difference between *it* as a reference item, as in line 27, and *it* as an impersonal subject, as in line 49 of Text 5.2. This difference in grammatical function can be confusing for some students.

Task 7

7.1 The definition of informal education in lines 24–5 is the closest in form to a naming definition (**can be called**).

7.2 Answers similar to the following would be acceptable:

Informal education may be defined as education which takes the form of learning by living or learning by doing.

If necessary, refer students again to the work done on formal definition in Unit 4, Tasks 5 and 14.

7.3 The formal definition suggested in 7.2 could then be extended by rewriting lines 22–4 so that they follow it:

This/Informal education takes place outside school, at home, on the street and on the job.

 # Text 5.2

Task 8

8.1 With less confident groups you may want to ask students initially to skim and identify the main ideas in the first paragraph only. They can then do the same with the next four paragraphs as a whole.

Task 9

9.2   (a) 2   (b) 4   (c) 1   (d) 3   (e) 5

Task 10

10.1 Three important assumptions underlying the debate in Asian universities up to the 1950s were:

1. All countries in Asia needed more scientists and technologists and would continue to do so for a long time to come (lines 4–8).

2. All countries in Asia would continue to emphasise the need for order and stability so that change could take place constructively (lines 8–11).

3. Traditional culture meant only those elements of it which were still living and meaningful to the lives of various Asian peoples (lines 11–14).

10.2 University leaders in Asia perceived this relationship as **close and meaningful** (lines 18–19). They also assumed that there was never a significant gulf between the culture which the Western society wanted to transmit and the values which the university promoted (lines 20–2). Furthermore, they felt it was arguable that even the rate of progress was always regulated by the interaction between the university and the other sectors of the community (line 22 ff).

10.3 The two main functions of the 'traditional university' in Asia were:

1. **to study, enrich and glorify traditional culture (including religious doctrine and practice)** (lines 33–4)

2. **(if they were secular) to train officials to preserve the traditional social and political order** (lines 35–6).

10.4 Lines 37–40 contain the most comprehensive statement of what modernising Asian leaders thought of the 'traditional university'. The emphasis in the next two sentences is slightly different. In lines 41–4 the subject is **the modern university**, and in lines 44–6 it is **Traditional culture**.

TASK 11

11.1   1. (a)   2. (c)   3. (b)   4. (b)   5. (a)   6. (b)   7. (c)

11.2
1. interplay
2. temporal
3. irreconcilable
4. outmoded
5. division
6. unrelated
7. undermining

TASK 12

Introduce the three categories of cohesive markers, and their sub-divisions. Then let the students work with the text to allocate each marker to its category.

12.1 The words can be grouped as follows, according to their connecting or cohesive functions:

1. AND type		2. BUT type	3. RELATIVE type
Summation	**Listing**	**Concession**	
therefore	For example	while	which
Thus	Another assumption	however	
	A third assumption	on the other hand	
		even though	
		In reality*	

* 'In reality' expresses a contradiction of a previous assertion and is often listed as **Equation** under an **AND** category, or as an **OR** type. It may be less confusing for students, however, to place it here.

12.2 You may want to go on to elicit further examples in each group and to add some under an **OR** category (**Reformulation** and **Replacement**).

> The extent to which you may want to sub-divide and describe connectives in technical terms will depend on the needs and proficiency of your class. You may want to simplify the process of describing the function of each group of connectives and limit the terminology to **AND**, **BUT**, **OR** and relative types. For fuller treatment of cohesive markers see the appendices to the Writing volume in this series. Refer your students to the appropriate section of a good students' grammar. e.g,:
>
> – Quirk, Greenbaum, Leech and Svartvik (1972) *A Grammar of Contemporary English*, Chapter 10, Longman. This gives a full list.
>
> – Woods, E. and McLeod, N. (1990) *Using English Grammar: Meaning and Form*, Section 5, Prentice Hall International.

Task 13

13.1 1. **The modernisers in Asia admired** … (Lines 28–30)
2. **This is putting the dichotomy in its simplest** … (Lines 47–9)
3. **In reality, the positions taken up** … (Lines 57–8)

13.2 **really** (line 59)

In the first instance the writer is emphasising the contrast between the over-simplified views held by many Asian leaders about the role of universities (lines 47–56) and the more varied positions taken up by the universities themselves on this issue (line 57 ff). In the second instance, the writer is stressing the ideal nature of the positions taken up by the many types of universities. In both cases there is a contrast between an initial appearance or impression and a more complex underlying reality

13.3 The writer is aware that a certain amount of simplification, perhaps even over-simplification, is necessary to give coherent and concise accounts of these complex situations or issues. He is also conscious, however, of the need to make it clear to readers that in each case the simplification can be misleading.

> You may want to point out to students that such reminders can often be necessary in their own academic writing to avoid the trap of sweeping statements or over-generalisations, especially if there is not enough evidence to warrant them.

TASK 14

14.1 The purpose of the final paragraph is to announce or signal a *transition* in the development of the discussion of two related topics. You can also refer again to the contrast outlined in Task 12 between the over-simplified views of Asian leaders on the role of universities and those held by the different types of universities.

14.2 We would expect the text to continue as the writer has predicted – that he will:

1. give an account of the varied positions taken up by the Asian universities on their role (lines 58–61)
2. then try to account for these positions by referring briefly to the historical establishment of universities in Asia (lines 61–3).

TASK 15

15.1 Both texts are written in a style which can be described as both formal and personal. Both writers maintain a consistently formal register but employ the first-person pronoun to refer to themselves: Text 5.1, line 13; Text 5.2, lines 58 and 61.

The complex sentence structures and formal vocabulary items are characteristic features of the academic styles seen in other texts in these units. You may want to refer to similar exercises on style in previous units, such as Units 1, 2 and 4.

> This would be a good opportunity to point out that although we teach students the orthodoxies of a written academic style which is both formal and impersonal, academic writers sometimes use first-person pronouns to refer to themselves in certain contexts, especially if they feel confident of their academic status or if the context of publication seems otherwise to warrant it. It would be best to prepare students to expect a variety of stylistic practices when they read academic texts, even if their subject tutors will expect them to maintain a consistently formal and impersonal style in their own writing.

15.2 Both texts were written for readers with specialist interests in education, sociology, economics or development studies. Text 5.1, however, is also intended for a more general readership and assumes less knowledge on the part of the reader.

15.3 Academic books or journals would be the most likely source of these.
Finance and Development, the source of Text 5.1, is not an academic journal in the strict sense, but in terms of both content and style it has many of the features of an academic journal. Articles are contributed by specialists in their fields.

TASK 16

16.1–2 Differences in educational and cultural background should raise some interesting differences of view on these topics. You may want to offer further discussion questions of your own.

TASK 17

17.1 You may want to devise related topics more suitable for the interests of your group. You may also want students to read or find other texts relating to those in this unit.
You can emphasise the structures of definition and extended definition introduced in Unit 4 and practised again here in relation to Text 5.1. Students can be asked to define key terms such as 'education', 'development' or 'a university' and to organise their essay on the basis of their extended definition. You may also want to give them more latitude in their approach to either topic.

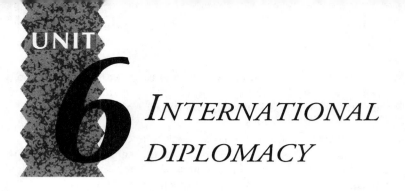

UNIT 6

INTERNATIONAL DIPLOMACY

PRE-READING TASK

A. You may want to elicit the students' understanding of *agenda* in the first instance. A simple definition is: a list of subjects to be talked about at a meeting. The term is used more abstractly and figuratively here, however, and so it comes to mean: a list of things to be dealt with, or a scheme of action.

 Text 6.1

TASK 1

1.1 The title refers to problems relating to the health of the planet. See lines 5–7.

TASK 2

2.1 Lines 5–7: **Now in the 1980s ...**

2.2 Lines 12–13: **New patterns of global management ...**

 Text 6.2

TASK 3

3.1 telephone, computer, aircraft, television, transport

3.2 Scanning.

TASK 4

4.1 therefore

4.2 The word in this context signals a logical conclusion (perhaps a conclusion that is being reiterated) from a previous stage of discussion. It also serves here as a marker of transition to the next stage of discussion.

The uses of *therefore* in drawing conclusions and in writing concluding paragraphs can be elicited or illustrated on the board/OHP.

TASK 5

5.2 Paragraph topics:

1. Expansion and greater complexity of diplomatic agenda after World War II.
2. New technology/telecommunications
   (a) speeded the transaction of business between nations
   (b) changed the conditions of decision-making.
3. Modern aircraft meant more frequent meetings of leaders, and raised level of conduct of inter-governmental business.
4. Television conveyed both words and pictures before diplomatic accounts of events could reach foreign ministries = public pressure.
5. Ease of travel meant greater government of people and aggravation of issues like minority rights, AIDS, terrorism.
6. More widespread narcotics problems in developed and developing countries = pressure to create interstate mechanisms to deal with them.

Similar answers are acceptable. You may want to give more concise versions of these topics.

5.3

Time period	Paragraph(s)	Lines
1988	1–2	1–10
1940s and 1950s (recent past)	2–5	10–46
the late 1980s	6	47–55

You can make the point here that the time periods provide some of the basis for the wider or global organisation of the text. You may also want to comment further on the time progression here:

> present
> distant past to recent past
> ↓ immediate past

This can be contrasted with a simpler and more strictly chronological organisation of time in narrative and descriptive accounts. It is worth mentioning that the first period represents a point in time, unlike the other two. The second period is a considerable expanse of time.

You may also want to draw attention to the different time specifications of **By 1988** in line 1 and **As the 1980s drew to a close** in line 47. The use of the past perfect in lines 1–9 can be contrasted with the simple past in the rest of the passage.

TASK 6

6.1   1. (b)   2. (a)   3. (c)   4. (b)   5. (a)   6. (c)

6.2   1. unilateral (antonym)   4. objective (synonym)
2. incursion (synonym)   5. improvement (antonym)
3. decelerated (antonym)   6. dispersion (synonym)

TASK 7

7.1 The left-hand column lists effects: the middle column lists causes.

Factors	Caused by development of	Lines
Increase in drug use	Travel, telephone	47–55
Global terrorism	Travel	42–6
Fewer records of conversations	Telephone	12–16
More ministerial-level meetings	Aircraft	22–9
Increase in speed of communications	Computer	16–18
Public pressure for prompt official statements/decisions	Television	30–5
Spread of disease	Travel	39–42
Difficulty of assessing importance of new information	Computer	18–21

You may want to remind students of the work done on cause and effect in Writing Unit 2.

Text 6.3

TASK 8

8.1 Text 6.3 is exceptionally long, and some students may feel daunted by the prospect of having to read it quickly. Emphasise that students should skim the text rapidly and not involve themselves in details. Five or six minutes should be enough. You may want to review the techniques of rapid reading in the chapter 'Introducing this book' before doing this task.

Answers can include some of the following points:

    (a) The solution to the impending environmental crisis will necessitate cooperation instead of competition between nation-states, and perhaps organisations which supersede the nation-state (lines 26–31).

    (b) The planet is increasingly over-crowded (lines 32–4).

    (c) The new agenda features the management of planetary environments, the protection of shared physical resources and global natural cycles (lines 54–9).

    (d) The new agenda has been shaped by issues affecting the health of the planet: availability of less harmful energy, pollution of the seas, ozone depletion, depletion of rain forests, the greenhouse effect, acid rain, waste disposal, famine in Africa, overpopulation (lines 60–121).

TASK 9

9.2 Lines 5–7:

    1. peace and war
    2. economic issues
    3. the transfer of resources from the richer to the poorer nations

9.3 Lines 19–31:

    1. Only a few nations have nuclear weapons but millions of people are involved in the destruction of the environment.

    2. Environmental disaster is caused by people doing things they feel are necessary, not by war.

    3. The solutions to environmental problems involve cooperation rather than competition between nation-states.

9.4   Barbara Ward   (line 34)
        Harland Cleveland   (line 39)
        Lincoln Bloomfield   (line 40)

They all agree that the world is near a state of crisis (lines 35–9 and 43–52). This crisis has environmental, political and economic aspects.

TASK 10

10.2
1. availability of less harmful energy (lines 63–6)
2. pollution of the seas (lines 73–8)
3. ozone depletion (lines 78–85)
4. depletion of rain forests (lines 86–91)
5. the greenhouse effect (lines 93–109)
6. acid rain (lines 60–2; 102)
7. waste disposal (lines 112–14)
8. famine in Africa (line 115)
9. overpopulation (lines 115–16)

10.3 Pollution of the Mediterranean (lines 74–8).

10.4 1985: Vienna. Convention for the Protection of the Ozone Layer (lines 83–4).
1987: Montreal. Conference on the ozone layer/reduction of fluorocarbons (lines 80–5).
1988: Rio de Janeiro. Conference on the depletion of tropical forests (lines 90–1).
1988: Toronto. Conference on 'The changing atmosphere' (lines 98–106).

TASK 11

11.1 1. (a)   2. (c)   3. (b)   4. (a)   5. (c)   6. (b)   7. (a)

11.2
1. essence
2. replace
3. foreshadowed
4. coastal
5. running down
6. deadly
7. wastefulness

TASK 12

12.1

Contrast between	Marker	Lines
1. environmental disaster/nuclear weapons decision	**unlike**	26–8
2. old problems/a new element	**but**	62–6
3. (global) environmental issues/solutions on national or regional basis	**but**	72–8

You may want to remind students here of the related work done on more systematic patterns of comparison/contrast in Reading Unit 3.

TASK 13

13.1 The main generalisations about **the new environmental agenda** are found in paragraph 4, lines 29–59.

Two of the specific issues on the agenda, however – acid rain and the availability of energy that will not damage the planet – are also introduced here.

13.2 The examples of specific environmental issues are found in paragraphs 6–9, lines 72–121.

The most commonly used structures and markers of exemplification are not found in these paragraphs, however. You may want to give further exercises on generalisation and exemplification to develop the students' understanding of this rhetorical function. It would also be useful to remind students of the work done on generalisation and qualification in Unit 1.

13.3 The writer will proceed to outline the **seven major problems** foreseen in 1988. These problems are in some way related to the **extravagance of [the planet's] inhabitants** (line 118).

TASK 14

14.1 A number of answers are possible here. Less confident students can use some of the material in the abstract (Text 6.1), if you feel it would help them. The sentence in lines 3–5 of Text 6.1 summarises Text 6.2, and the two sentences in lines 5–10 summarise Text 6.3. Students would still need to incorporate more details to write a paragraph of 8–10 sentences, however.

The following paragraph includes most of the major ideas:

> By 1988 the work of international diplomacy had expanded and become more complex because of the increased number of nation-states and the more multilateral nature of diplomacy. New developments in technology and communications had accelerated the transaction of business between nations and changed the conditions of decision-making. Policy-makers found it necessary to assess greatly increased amounts of information. The speed of travel raised the level at which inter-governmental business was conducted. More widespread travel aggravated issues such as minority rights, the dissemination of diseases and drugs. Linked with these changes was a new environmental agenda, once the threat of nuclear war had subsided. The greenhouse effect, acid rain, pollution, the destruction of rain forests and famine all became issues of concern on a global scale in a world of increasingly interdependent nations. Political leaders and diplomats will find these problems difficult to control and negotiate.

This exercise is designed to give students practice in the skills of synthesising and summarising information from more than one text, skills which will be important in their academic writing once they begin their degree courses. This exercise corresponds with similar exercises in Unit 6 of the Writing book in this series and can be used to prepare students for Writing Unit 6.

In Task 5.2 students identified the main ideas or topics in each paragraph of Text 6.2. You may want to refer them again to the chapter 'Introducing this book' in the Student's Book to elicit strategies for identifying the most important ideas in Text 6.3. These strategies correspond with the strategies for skimming outlined there. The main ideas or topics in Texts 6.2 and 6.3, once identified by the students, can serve as the basis of their synthesis and summary.

TASK 15

15.1–2 The discussion may raise some interesting differences of perspective on this subject, particularly from students who live in countries in which the communications revolution has made fewer inroads.

The discussion may also raise some contentious issues relating to the vested interests behind these worldwide changes. Multinational corporations involved in communications technology wield considerable power. Some groups may want to consider the implications of this.

TASK 16

16.1 Students can be given a relatively free hand with this essay topic. You may prefer to devise a related topic more suitable to the interests of your group. You may also want students to read or find other texts relating to those in this unit.

If students seem able and willing to produce the **Situation→Problem→Solution→Evaluation** pattern in their writing at this point, they can be encouraged to use it in their essays and to plan their writing accordingly.

Some may feel that they would like to organise the essay in a different way, however. They can be encouraged to do so if you feel they have already had sufficient practice in producing this pattern of organisation, or if you intend to proceed to Unit 6 in the Writing book in this series. An opportunity to practise using this pattern of organisation is given in Unit 4. More sustained practice in producing this is given in Writing Units 4 and 6 in this series.

UNIT 7

DEVELOPMENT AND CULTURAL VALUES IN AFRICA

 Text 7.1

TASK 1

1.1 Some students may find it difficult to identify the overall idea in Text 7.1 after rapid reading, in part because of the complexity of some of the sentences. You can refer them especially to lines 6–13 and 14–21. A second, more selective, skimming of these lines only may help.

TASK 2

2.2 The dominant purpose of *persuasion* is evident here, especially in the lines referred to above in Task 1 (lines 6–13 and 14–21). See also 6.3, in which students are asked to recognise that this is an essay of *formal argument*.

2.3 The thesis is contained in lines 14–21. The verb signalling this is **argues** (line 17).

2.4 If students have difficulty with this, they can be asked to explain lines 17–21 only. The long, complex sentence structure and involved parenthesis may cause initial comprehension problems for some students.

2.5 The writer claims authoritative support for his thesis on the following basis:

1. It is based on his own work, which implies research (line 14).
2. It is based on published and unpublished studies and research on the economic psychology of Sub-Saharan ethnic groups (lines 14–17).
3. The thinking behind it forms the basis of a study undertaken by the World Bank (lines 21–30).

See Task 13, in which the question of evidence is explored further in terms of degree of certainty.

Task 3

3.1 The most important contrast in the first paragraph of Text 7.1 is found in lines 6 ff. Traditional approaches to development, which fail to take account of indigenous cultural values, are implied in lines 4–6 and explicitly stated in lines 10–13. These are contrasted with the opposing view that success can only be achieved by integrating into economic decision-making the political and sociocultural values that operate at a local level.

3.2 **however** (line 7).

3.3 **decades of efforts** (line 4) = distant past – recent past
Recently (line 6) = recent past – present

The contrast in time periods here helps to emphasise the contrast in points of view about development. It also gives further weight to the implication that the previous view may become outmoded, especially since it has also met with **limited success**.

In this case, however, the contrast in time periods is not signalled by differences in verb tenses. Both sentences use the present perfect, presumably because the traditional view of development is still current among other development specialists.

Task 4

4.1 1. (c)   2. (b)   3. (c)   4. (a)   5. (c)   6. (b)

4.2 1. benefactor   3. do wrong   5. inducement
        2. assumption   4. direction   6. lasting

Task 5

5.1 (a) **the poor performance of the public sector and chronic weaknesses in the local institutions** (lines 2–4)

(b) the limited success of efforts to change the situation outlined in lines 2–4.

(c) that the problem arises from **a failure … to integrate political and sociocultural values in the process of economic decision-making** (lines 8–10).

(d) **the main body of development literature** (lines 10–11).

(e) **this essay** (line 14)

(f) **a study recently begun by the World Bank** (lines 21–2).

TASK 6

6.1 The writer refers to himself in line 14 as **the author** and in lines 30 and 31 as **we**. A similar form of reference would be 'the writer/the present writer'.

You may want to advise students to consult their subject tutors on their academic courses about the preferred form of referring to oneself. Some may advise against the use of 'we'.

6.2 Formal and impersonal. Specific features can be given as follows:

    (a) The author avoids the use of the first person singular in referring to himself.

    (b) The text contains a number of long, complex sentence structures characteristic of formal, academic writing. See especially lines 14–21.

    (c) The writer's use of vocabulary is consistently formal in its register. You can refer in the first paragraph, for example, to terms such as **sociocultural values** (line 9), **premise** (line 10), and **an obstacle to institutional and technical innovations** (lines 12–13). The only exception to this is the more informal phrase, **to turn this situation around** (line 5).

You may want to ask students to select further items of formal vocabulary from the second paragraph, and discuss aspects of the usefulness of such language: abstraction, comprehensive applicability, objectivity, need to distance self from the information, etc.

6.3 These paragraphs introduce an essay of formal argument.

The writer's intention to persuade is very evident in the first paragraph. This is followed by the clear presentation of a thesis (lines 14–21) which he maintains is supported by evidence (lines 14–17) and the authority of the World Bank (lines 21–30). Moreover, as students have seen in 6.2, the writer's use of language is consistently formal.

 # Text 7.2

TASK 7

7.1 With less proficient groups you may want to divide the text into two parts for skimming. Lines 34–50 and 85–92 can be skimmed first for the overall idea. Students can then skim the intervening lines, 51–84, in which the author outlines his counter-arguments.

TASK 8

8.2 The three most important assumptions of traditional development projects are:

1. an understanding of history and development which assumes that every society must undergo the same stages of economic and technological progress (lines 35–7)

2. an approach to development and management which assumes that Western, technologically-oriented methods are the only valid ways of reaching 'modernisation' (lines 37–40)

3. an assumption that other countries should adopt Western value systems to achieve development (lines 40–5).

8.3 The logical conclusion of these assumptions is that Africa's development needs to be stimulated from the 'outside' and not from 'inside' its own systems of methods and values.

8.4 He disagrees with all three assumptions (lines 49–50).

TASK 9

9.1   1. (c)   2. (b)   3. (c)   4. (a)   5. (b)   6. (a)

9.2   1. power   3. corresponding   5. surpass
         2. ideal   4. tribalism   6. peculiarity

TASK 10

10.1 There are three counter-arguments, one for each of the assumptions described in lines 34–45:

1. The success of the informal sector in Africa, which reconciles economic efficiency with African social and cultural values, points to the limitations of **the linear conception** (lines 51–9).

2. The input of technology is not enough: there must also be a high degree of national identification with and widespread commitment to a project for it to work.

3. Western value systems are not always consistent with those in Africa, where family and ethnic loyalty are usually more important than self-reliance, self-interest and even national interest.

10.2   **First** (line 51)
    Second (line 60)
    Third (line 71)

You may want to point out that these connecting words or markers of sequential transition are emphasised by their placement at the opening of each paragraph. These signals are particularly clear and emphatic here, but it may be as well to advise students not to expect such emphatic clarity in all of their reading texts.

TASK 11

11.1 If institutional development in Africa is to be effective, technical–managerial elements will have to be integrated with the distinctive features of African political and sociocultural structures (lines 85–92).

11.2 **Thus** (line 85).

TASK 12

12.1   1. Three key assumptions of traditional development programmes.
   2. The conclusion of traditional assumptions is that Africa's development must be stimulated from outside. But the evidence contradicts these assumptions.
   3. Limits of the linear conception of development: the success of the informal sector in Africa.
   4. Limits of the technological approach: there must also be a high degree of 'internalisation' of projects.
   5. Western values are not always consistent with motivations and behaviour patterns prevalent in Africa.
   6. The distinctive features of African political and sociocultural structures must be understood and integrated into development programmes.

TASK 13

In relation to Task 13, it would be helpful to discuss the importance in academic texts generally of the following considerations in assessing the reliability of evidence and the degree of certainty that is warranted by it:

   1. How authoritative does the source seem to be?
   2. Is specific evidence cited by the source?

3. How much has the evidence been evaluated, by the source or by the writer referring to it (if at all)?

4. How conclusively is the evidence given by the source interpreted or put forward by the writer (e.g. the different degrees of certainty expressed in 'suggests', 'supports', 'shows', 'proves', etc.)?

5. Have the conclusions reached by one source been confirmed by independent evidence from another source?

For purposes of academic study students will need to practise this analytical awareness in both their reading and their writing.

13.1   (b) 3/4   (c) 4/5   (d) 1   (e) 5   (f) 2

The suggested answers here are approximate. The scale is designed to help students avoid 'black-and-white', true/false over-simplifications about the reliability of information from sources and to think about arguments and evidence in terms of *degree of certainty*.

Discussion of the implications of key words in each expression would be useful. You may want to place on the board /OHP a scale similar to the following:

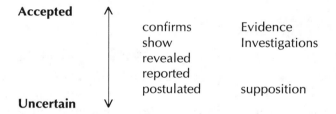

Accepted	↑		
		confirms	Evidence
		show	Investigations
		revealed	
		reported	
		postulated	supposition
Uncertain	↓		

Other words of this kind could then be elicited and placed on the scale, for example:

hypothesis   research   evaluation of data
suggests   demonstrates   proves

13.2 The writer gives two basic sources of evidence for his ideas in Text 7.1:

1. It is based on his own work, which implies research (line 14).
2. It is based on published and unpublished studies and research on the economic psychology of Sub-Saharan ethnic groups (lines 14–17).

You may want to take this further by posing the question of whether or not we should take these claims at face value. Unless specific sources are cited somewhere in the article to support claim 2, we are entitled to question their validity. In fact, only one specific source is cited in the original article: 'For a fuller discussion of the economic psychology of African tribes, see *Psychologie Economique Africaine* by Jacques Binet, Payot, Paris, 1970.' We can at least wonder whether there are more up-to-date sources available on this subject.

On the other hand, a full list of sources would not be expected in a text of this kind. It is written in a relatively formal academic style but is not intended exclusively for specialists or academics.

13.3   (a) 3/4   (b) 4   (c) 4/5   (d) 3

Again, the suggested answers here are approximate.

13.4   The second counter-argument, lines 60–70, is presented with the greatest degree of certainty. This is consistently maintained in the paragraph:

> **clearly shows ...** (line 61)
> **it is now generally accepted that ... will not suffice** (lines 62–5)
> **There must also be ...** (line 66)

13.5   The third counter-argument, lines 71–84, is presented with the lowest degree of certainty. This is consistently maintained, with the possible exception of line 81:

> **seem to suggest that ... are not always congruent with ...** (lines 72–3)
> **tend to ...** (line 75)
> **seems to be ...** (line 77)
> **Generally ... takes precedence ...** (lines 79–80)
> **Clearly ... were simply not long enough ...** (line 81)

13.6   The third counter-argument is supported by **extensive studies and research** (line 71). It is likely that the others have corresponding forms of support, but they are not specifically cited here.

Students may ask why this third counter-argument is put forward with the least degree of certainty, when it is supported by research findings. This is not entirely clear. It may be that the findings have yet to be evaluated or confirmed.

Task 14

14.1   Paragraph 1 (lines 1–13) of Text 7.1 introduces the article as a whole. It is *similar* to paragraphs 3–8 (Text 7.2) because it contains in condensed form most of the main ideas there. It is *different* in that it develops these main ideas with much more information and supporting evidence. Text 7.2 also outlines three counter-arguments to the assumptions of traditional development programmes which are not specifically mentioned in paragraph 1.

14.2   The writer has organised the text in this way in order to create an effective introduction which:

> (a) leads into the essay
> (b) outlines many of the main ideas to be developed in the following paragraphs.

The main ideas found in the introduction are taken up and developed more fully later in the text. You may want to point out to students that the coherence of the organisation illustrated in this text is something they should try to achieve in their own academic writing.

This may also be a good opportunity to discuss the function and importance of introductions in reading texts as well as in writing academic essays. Refer students again to the chapter 'Introducing this book' in the Student's Book. The extent to which introductions present the main ideas in a text can vary considerably.

TASK 15

15.2 The second discussion question focuses on some of the fundamental assumptions about development and questions whether it can be considered exclusively in material terms. Students from non-Western countries may be able to contribute some interesting ideas here.

TASK 16

16.1 Students can be given a relatively free hand with this essay topic. You may want to devise a related topic more suitable for the interests of your group. You may also want students to read or find other texts relating to those in this unit.

You could emphasise the structure of formal argument used by the writer in the reading texts. Students can be asked to follow a similar pattern in which the thesis is stated clearly and then supported systematically by further ideas and evidence. However, if you intend to go on to do the corresponding unit in the Writing course in this series, you may want to suggest a more open-ended approach to this essay.